Hatch

Hatch

21 Day Journey to Self-Discovery
Unleashing the Authentic You

Fernandos L. Harrington Jr.

Foreword by Veronica J. Glover

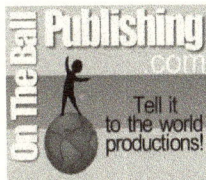

On The Ball Publishing.com

Tell it
to the world
productions!

Edmond, OK

Hatch

Cover Design by: Eudora L. Harrington © 2014
Author's Photo by: Eudora L. Harrington © 2015

ISBN (paperback): 978-0-9834341-6-0
Library of Congress Control Number: 2015907914

First Edition

For permissions, write to On The Ball Publishing LLC
PO Box 6982, Edmond, OK 73083-6982

www.ontheballpublishing.com

Printed in the United States of America

Contents

2001, I wrote a program titled, *Project: Changing Focus.* It was a multi-component program designed to help others reach their dreams and goals. It served as the springboard to what would later lead to speaking engagements and the program is used in schools in the community. However, there was something or "some things" lacking.

When I approached Fernandos, my younger brother, he asked me, "How bad do you want it?" I knew I wanted it quite badly, but before I could answer, he answered for me, "Get in alignment, sis." I never doubted what he said to be truth. I never doubted that he was genuine and I never doubted his concern for my success. That was exactly what I needed, an alignment.

With this book, you will start to align yourself with the principles of success. Fernandos' book represents that steadfast, unmovable nature that never stops to look back. Unquestionably, there is no doubt about the uniqueness and strength that this book has to offer.

When life gives us lemons, we should make lemonade, right? You cannot do this without the tools you need—tools such as having a plan of action and referring back to the owner's manual.

Through his daily, thought-provoking questions and action steps, Fernandos offers you very timely solutions for operating in today's busy world. This book is real. As you read, from "Day 1" through "Day 21", *Hatch* speaks directly to the heart—that inner child that will always live inside of each and every one of us.

When Fernandos is not certain about something he says so. He allows his readers to be the final judge as he unfailingly refers back to his owner's manual wherein all the details and truth lies. His unstoppable nature shines on every page, particularly when he gently commands you to step outside the box in your thoughts and actions.

This is a remarkable book, a reference source and an action plan rolled into one. It is a single bright light that cuts across the sometimes dark pages of our lives. This book will be used every day by folks interested in true success. This book is for all of us who continue to strive for success in our lives and for those of us who have ever wanted to, this book is right for you. Embrace the challenge *now*! For nothing is more worthy than starting today.

Thank you, Fernandos L. Harrington Jr. I never doubted that you could do this—not then, not now and not for a minute did I doubt.

By Veronica J. Glover

Author, Educator, Business Manager, and Entrepreneur

This book was written for the person who knows that there is more to life than their current situation; the person who is stuck between who they are and who they are becoming; the person who may be confused and lost about the direction in which their life is going; or the person who has ever asked the question, why did God create me?

I pray that the words from this book become alive in your heart—igniting the purpose of God in you. Read each day at the beginning of your day in a quiet place and answer the questions truthfully. There are no wrong answers! As you read, the next 21 days of your life will be your launching pad for bigger and better things to come.

My Prayer for You

Father, I pray for everyone whom has a copy of this book; that you will open each soul, mind, and heart to receive what you have already planned for each of their extraordinary lives. And that every reader of this book agrees with who you made each of them to be. Let your journey begin! In Jesus' name I pray. Amen.

Acknowledgements

To my wife, Chandra, of over 16 years, thanks for supporting and loving me through all of my wild and crazy ideas. I know it's not easy being married to a person like me but you're great at it! Because of your love, support and encouragement, I was able to write this book.

Thanks also to my family and friends for all of their love and support. You guys rock! A special thanks to my three sons, Zechariah, Joshua and Caleb Harrington because you three gave daddy a broader perspective on life that I will be forever thankful for.

Day 1

Success

When you think of the word success, what comes to your mind? Some of you may think that success is having lots of money, being at the top of your profession or owning your own business. Whatever your definition of success, there are three things you must consider when achieving success:

1. **Success** is a personal choice. Nobody can make you want to be successful.

2. **Success** always involves standards. So you must consider who or what is choosing your standards.

3. **Success** always comes with a cost. You must be willing to pay full price because success never goes on sale.

Questions:

1. Do you choose to be successful?

2. How do you define success?

_____

_____

_____

_____

_____

_____

3. What standards does your success live by?

_____

_____

_____

_____

_____

_____

4. What price are you willing to pay and not pay to make

   success your reality?

   _____

   _____

   _____

   _____

   _____

Day 2

Channel Surfing

Picture yourself sitting at home relaxing on your couch. You pick up the remote control to turn on your television. You begin to take interest in what you're seeing. Now, without any notice, you lose interest. So…what do you do? You change the channel until you come across a program you want to watch. My point is that your mind (thoughts) is the remote control to your life. If you don't like what you see, change your channel. Whatever you habitually think about, you become! According to Proverbs 23:7, "For as he thinketh in his heart, so is he…"

Action Plan:

1. Make a conscious decision today to govern your thoughts. Write down steps you can take to help assist you in this process.

2. Write a list of statements that declare the truth about who

GOD created you to be. Repeat these three times daily.

_____

_____

_____

_____

_____

_____

_____

_____

_____

_____

_____

_____

_____

_____

_____

_____

_____

_____

3. If any negative thoughts come to your mind, repeat the

statements that you listed in step two.

Day 3

Thinking

Have you ever unconsciously or consciously thought something about yourself over and over again? Then, without notice you found yourself believing it (whether good or bad) and that thought became your reality. This is the power of your thinking! Whatever you think about and whatever you talk about is actually producing life or death in you. You must remember that life or death is in the power of your tongue. Whatever you speak will become your reality! Take a few minutes to answer the following questions.

Questions:

1. What do you think about the most?

_____

_____

_____

_____

2. Do you speak life (positive things, truth) over yourself, your family and others?

_____

_____

_____

_____

_____

_____

3. What can you do to create a new thought habit?

_____

_____

_____

_____

_____

Day 4

I Can, I Will, I Must

So many people desire to be successful and they desire to be great, but they never move past the phrase, "I can." You see, "I can" is just the beginning phase of achieving purpose. It is the first conscious decision that you make in your mind that says, "I can do this." Every great fulfillment in life always starts with the phrase, "I can." However, you must then graduate to the phrase "I will!" The "I will" of a person is hammering out the details of what it is that you can do, but in order to achieve purpose in your life, you have to move to a reality in your mind ... from "I can and I will" to "I MUST!" What this means is that you give yourself no other option in life but to fulfill your true purpose. Take flight today!

Questions:

As you respond to the following questions, write down what you think God's purpose is for you to do. Here are four keys to think about:

1. Read your owner's manual (Holy Bible). A car doesn't know why it was created. You must call the manufacturer or read the owner's manual. Meditate on Genesis 1:26-28. There, you will find God's purpose for creating mankind.

_____

_____

_____

_____

2. What are you passionate about? Your passion will always lead you to your specific purpose.

_____

_____

_____

_____

3. What are some things you would do for free? There aren't

    too many things people would do for free.

_____

_____

_____

_____

_____

_____

_____

4. What brings you joy?

_____

_____

_____

_____

_____

_____

Day 5

Your Garden

Imagine that it's spring, and the sun is out. There's a light breeze and the temperature is perfect. You're walking and enjoying a perfect 85 degree day. Suddenly, you come upon a beautiful garden. It's colorful, groomed and not a weed in sight. You stop to talk to the owner to inquire about how he was able to produce such a breath taking garden. The answer was simple. I planted the right seeds, in the right soil with the right care and it produced this beautiful garden.

Your mind is like that beautiful fertile garden. Whatever you plant, will grow. What are you planting in your garden? Are you planting fear, doubt, strife or negativity? Or, are you planting love, joy, success, prosperity and truth? It's your garden. You have to make the choice what you want to plant.

Action Plan:

Meditate on this today and become conscious of what you

think about all day. Write down your thoughts and take a

look at your list before you go to bed. If your thoughts don't

align with the truth that God says about you, create new

thoughts that do. Refer back to day two and your list of what

you believe God created you to be and write your responses

below:

_____

_____

_____

_____

_____

_____

Day 6

Your Thinking

Yesterday, I asked you to journal all of your thoughts. Today, I'm going to tell you what the Bible says about them. It says, "Finally, brethren, whatsoever things are true, whatsoever things are honest, whatsoever things are just, whatsoever things are pure, whatsoever things are lovely, whatsoever things are of good report; if there be any virtue, and if there be any praise, think on these things" (Philippians 4:8). Don't waste your time thinking on negativity. Start taking the time to think on things that have a good report. Remember, "…as he thinketh in his heart, so is he…"

Question:

1. Think of 10 good things you can say about yourself right now. Now, put *"I am"* in front of them and write them down below. Then, each day go through the list you have written and read your list out loud.

_____

_____

_____

_____

_____

_____

_____

_____

_____

Day 7

You Get What You Expect

Remember when you were a kid and your parents promised you that on Saturday, they would take you skating? All week leading up to that Saturday, you talked about it. You told everyone you could that you were going skating. Not only did you talk about it, you made sure all of your actions were in alignment, giving your parents no reason to change their minds. You did all of this because you believed what your parents told you and you expected it to happen. Our faith in God is not just saying we believe in God.

Faith is having an expectation of what God says you can have and aligning your actions with that expectation even though you don't have all the details. Whatever you expect to happen in your life, align your actions to it and trust God. In the book of Hebrew 11:1, it says, "Now faith is the substance of things hoped for, the evidence of things not seen."

Hope is your end result. Your faith is what goes to work to make hope your reality. Without hope, your faith is unemployed! Take some time to answer these three questions.

Questions:

1. What are you expecting God to do in your life (not what you want him to do in your life)? There is a difference.

_____

_____

_____

2. What have you done to align yourself with that expectation?

_____

_____

_____

3. How are you measuring the results of your alignment to

your expectation?

_____

_____

_____

_____

_____

_____

_____

_____

_____

_____

_____

Day 8

Do You Have The Right

Hunger?

In the story of Esau and Jacob, Esau sold his birthrights for a bowl of stew because his hunger took priority. Have you ever been so hungry that you would give anything to satisfy that hunger? Hunger in and of itself is never bad, but you must be careful what you hunger for. If you crave riches, power, fame, or acceptance, you might be selling your birthrights to get it. Peace, prosperity, love and joy are what we should hunger for. Read Genesis 25: 29-34 and answer the following question.

Question:

What are some of the key points of this story that stand out to you? As you write your responses, let the words speak to you and think about how you can apply it to your life today.

_____

_____

_____

_____

_____

_____

_____

_____

Hatch

Day 9

Planning

The stage has been set. The date and time has been appointed. You have been telling everyone you know about this great event. The anticipation sets in. The crowds start to arrive in record numbers. Your team shows up and they are ready for the next move. They ask you, "What's the plan?" Your response is, "What plan?" They look at you in utter disbelief because the greatest event is now going to fail because of lack of planning. Sound familiar? Isn't this how it goes in your life? You talked about all the great things you wanted to do and when you want to do them. You get super excited anticipating when they will happen, but you leave out one small detail, a plan. Many of us plan to fail because we never plan at all! Get your vision from GOD and build your life accordingly. Get a plan of action and take action. Ready. Set. Go!

Questions:

1. What is your vision/mission statement for your life? Write

   it down. Memorize it and meditate on it daily.

   _____

   _____

   _____

   _____

   _____

2. What steps do you plan to take to get there?

   _____

   _____

   _____

   _____

   _____

_____

_____

_____

_____

_____

_____

_____

3. Repeat those steps daily to yourself and take action until

it's accomplished. NOW (No Opportunity Wasted)

is your time!

Day 10

Free Yourself

Think about this. You and someone you know are tied up and trapped in a closet. You begin to tell that person how to get free and you then start trying to help free this person. The only problem is that you are tied up and trapped also. Are you getting the picture? This is what we do in our everyday lives with our relationships with people. We try to untie and loose others when we are not loosed ourselves. You cannot liberate another without first liberating yourself. Stop focusing on what others are doing and saying. It has no direct impact on your *destiny* unless you let it. Free your *mind! Think* differently. *Live* differently!

Time to Meditate:

Stop right now. Clear your mind and relax. Move all thoughts out of your head, open your hands with your palms facing upward and repeat, "I take full responsibility for what I've done in life and what I've done is not who I am. I am fearfully and wonderfully made. I have a divine purpose to fulfill and nobody can stop me from fulfilling my *purpose,* not even me. I give myself permission to become the person that God fully created me to be and I receive the prosperity of God in life."

Repeat this statement three times a day (morning, noon and before bed).

Day 11

What's Stopping You?

Imagine that you have just been left a million dollar inheritance. The person that left it to you has already done the paperwork for you to receive it. All you have to do is go and claim it. You tell yourself, "I will go tomorrow" and tomorrow come and you don't go. So, you tell yourself that you'll go next week. Well you get the point. You keep putting it off, but you consistently struggle to keep your head above water.

You have an unlimited inheritance left to you by the Father. All you have to do is claim it! Procrastination is nothing more than a dream killer in slow-motion! Believe in the God who put the dream in you, believe in yourself and *take action*. You can do it!

Questions:

1. What are you going to do today that brings you closer to

   accomplishing your dream?

---

2. What are the steps you are going to take to ensure you do

    it?

_____

_____

_____

_____

_____

_____

_____

_____

_____

_____

_____

Hatch

Day 12

Can You See Your

Opportunity?

✝

Your alarm goes off. You hit the snooze button only to awaken one hour past the time you were supposed to get up. Now, you are in a frenzy. You are rushing to try and get things done at a rapid speed. Just when you think you're gaining ground on the time you lost, the phone rings. It's some   disappointing news. You rush out the door only to find you have a flat tire. You say to yourself, "I am having a bad day."

We all have experienced this at some time or another in our life, but the truth is that it's not a bad day, but how you have perceived your day to be. Your day is what you make of it. Problems and opposition are nothing more than an *opportunity*. Seize your moment! Your promotion is in your problem!

Time to Meditate:

Today, take the time to look at all the things you think are problems and opposition in your life. Then write down solutions to what you perceive to be your problems. Seize your moment of opportunity *today*! To help you get started, first read Daniel 2:12-18.

_____

_____

_____

_____

_____

_____

_____

_____

Day 13

Knowing You

Have you ever wondered why animals are so effective at what they do? A dog barks and chases cars. A cat purrs and a rabbit hops. You get the point. They do these very effectively because the dog never tries to be the cat and the cat never tries to be the dog. They know who they are!

Do you wonder what would happen if you get to know who you are? Knowing *you* is the biggest part of your success. Don't try to be something you're not. Learn your strengths and weaknesses. Expose your strengths. Work on your weaknesses. You are fearfully and wonderfully made. Nobody on the planet can beat you at being you. Practice being you today!

Action Plan:

1. Write down all of your strengths.

_____

_____

_____

_____

_____

_____

2. Identify your weaknesses.

_____

_____

_____

_____

_____

Now from these two lists, choose today to focus on just one of your strengths and work on correcting one of your weaknesses. Put it into action today. Practice daily on becoming the person God created you to be!

Day 14

Don't Get Comfortable

Getting paid to do what you love is an extraordinary feat. For example, look at professional athletes. They get millions to play a game. The extraordinary ones get paid multimillions. What is it that great players know that the others don't? The great ones understand that just because you make it on that level, doesn't mean you're guaranteed to stay on that level. You see, some of the athletes get comfortable with their level of achievement and success. Who wouldn't do the same? After all, only one percent of all college students even make it on the pro level in sports. So, it is a very big achievement when they reach this level of success. But then these players get accustomed to the salary and lifestyle, never putting any more time into perfecting their gift. Suddenly, they find themselves like every other player on that level, just blending in and getting by. Sound familiar? Comfort will always make you mediocre and mediocre means common. God didn't create you to be common. He intentionally created you to be *great!* Embrace discomfort. Greatness is born from it.

Questions:

1. Examine your life. Are you comfortable?

_____

2. Do you want more in life? If so, what?

_____

_____

_____

_____

_____

3. What is stopping you from achieving it?

_____

_____

_____

_____

_____

_____

_____

_____

_____

4. What is God making uncomfortable in your life? What is

   He making GREAT in you through the process?

_____

_____

_____

_____

Day 15

Thought Process

Where you are in life is a direct impact on what you think. What you think has a direct impact on what you speak. What you speak has a direct impact on what you believe. What you believe has a direct impact on what you have been exposed to. What you have been exposed to has a direct impact on your environment and your environment has a direct impact on your choices. Choose an environment that will expose you to the truth so that you may start believing, thinking and speaking the *truth* about who you were created to be. Dare to be you!

Questions:

1. What are your thought habits? Become aware of what you think about all day.

_____

_____

_____

_____

_____

_____

_____

_____

_____

2. What are you feeding your mind on a day-to-day basis? What do you watch on TV? What do you listen to on the radio? What do you talk about with your friends?

_____

_____

_____

_____

Day 16

Watch Your Words

Today, our lives are so busy. We live in a world where everything is quick, fast and in a hurry. Have you ever skipped breakfast; ran out of the door only to find out later when you got to work as the morning moved along your stomach starts to signal you that it's hungry? Sooner or later, you will find out that skipping breakfast is not a good idea because it sets the physical tone for your whole day.

Well, I'm here to tell you that the words that you say to yourself first thing in the morning do the same thing. Your words can either create an atmosphere of positivity, love, and peace or an atmosphere of negativity, fear, and worry. Command your morning! Remember, upon rising every day, speak life to yourself everyday of your life. After all, life and death are in your tongue. Your words are powerful, so be conscious of what you speak.

Action Plan:

Grab your Bible. Go through your Bible and write down as many promises as you can find that God has made to you. Now, repeat those over you and your family every morning and night.

_____

_____

_____

_____

_____

_____

_____

_____

Day 17

Control Your Feelings

In Genesis 27, Jacob comes in to receive the blessings from Isaac, his father. Isaac says to him, "You sound like Jacob but you feel like Esau." Then, Isaac proceeds to bless him. Isaac made a permanent decision based on what he felt and not what he heard! Do not make a permanent decision based on temporary feelings. Listen to the small still voice inside of you.

Questions:

1. What are some of the choices you've made based on feelings?

_____

_____

_____

_____

2. What did you learn from those experiences?

_____

_____

_____

_____

_____

_____

3. What is God saying to you right now that you need to

obey?

_____

_____

_____

_____

Day 18

Creativity

As a little kid, I used to love when the teacher would give us a blank sheet of paper and tell us to draw what we see. She would say, "Imagine that you could be anything in the world. What would that be?" I would start to draw and my imagination would run wild. Even as a kid, I can remember having a very big imagination and although some people might not have understood my drawings, I knew exactly what I was drawing because I saw it in my head. Although my creativity was different than the other kids, I still had the ability to create what I saw.

That blank sheet of paper represents your life and you have the ability to create anything you want because you were created by a Creator. That means you can recreate what God has already created for you to have. Life and death are in your tongue.

Questions

1. What does creativity mean to you?

_____

_____

_____

_____

_____

_____

2. What do you need to create in your life now?

_____

_____

_____

_____

_____

3. How are you going to create it?

_____

_____

_____

_____

_____

_____

_____

_____

_____

_____

_____

_____

Day 19

Throw Yourself A Party

$\backsim\!\!\times$

Accomplishing a goal or task is a big deal. It takes focus, commitment, and discipline. Most people are so blinded by the vision they forget to celebrate when they reach certain milestones along the way. Don't forget to celebrate your own accomplishments. Whenever you take a step towards fulfilling your purpose, no matter how small or big, just remember you are a step closer to achieving it. Encourage yourself today. Stay focused. Stay committed. You are almost there!

Action Plan:

Give yourself a hug and tell yourself, "I'm proud of you." How did that make you feel?

_____

_____

Day 20

The Process Is Important

Life throws all types of challenges and puts all types of obstacles in your way. Sometimes, we can get discouraged along the way because the process of achieving our goal just seems too hard. Gold doesn't turn into gold without enduring a process. You see, it's the process that gives the gold it's shiny, glossy finish by burning out all the impurities. Without process, there can be no promise! Remember that the process and promise go hand in hand. If you abort your process, then you will kill your promise.

Questions:

1. What process are you going through at this time in your life?

_____

_____

_____

2. How are you handling this process?

_____

_____

_____

_____

_____

_____

_____

3. What's the promise connected to your process?

_____

_____

_____

_____

_____

Day 21

It's In You!

Create the Action Plan:

Go back through your devotional book and read what you have written. Create a plan of action on how you're going to accomplish these things. Remember, your plan has to be sound and practical. Never compromise your dreams. Always be willing to change your thinking and your plans.

I will now close this book by speaking life into you.

"Father I pray for the person that's reading this book right now. I ask that you awaken their inner greatness and that you open their eyes to see all that you placed inside of them; that they may take action *now*! I speak to their mind; that it's renewed by the truth. I speak prosperity over their life. I speak wealth over their money. I command their family to be in perfect harmony, peace, and love. Most of all, Father, I Pray that if they don't know you that you will save them now in Jesus' name. Amen!"

If you want to know Christ as your Lord and Savior, say these words out loud, "Lord, I believe that Christ died on the cross for my sins because I am a sinner. I make you, Lord of my life this day. Thank you for your saving grace. In Jesus' name I pray. Amen!"

It's important that you surround yourself with other strong believers and start reading the Word! Welcome to your new life in Christ Jesus.

About the Author

Fernandos L. Harrington Jr. (F.L.) is an entrepreneur, author, pastor, elite certified life coach, and public speaker. With his unique set of skills and gifting, he provides life-changing insight into the lives of many. Beginning at the age of sixteen, he owned and sold several businesses. He developed his cleaning business into a company with annual revenue grossing six-figures in just twenty-four months. In addition to his traditional education at Southwestern Christian University, F.L. is certified as an Elite Life Coach. He and his wife, Chandra, of over sixteen years, are proud parents of three boys; Zechariah, Joshua, and Caleb. Joshua went home to be with God just a few hours after he was born. Through intense struggles and tests like these, God prepared F.L. and Chandra for their ministry whereby they actively serve people in the community with a focus on meeting individuals' needs and elevating their lives through God's purpose. His love and passion for people, for life, and for God's Word has enhanced his coaching, his public speaking, and his ministry. F.L.'s ministry enables him to influence and empower many to achieve ultimate fulfillment by discovering, clarifying, and taking action toward fulfilling their life's purpose. F.L.'s purpose is simple—to interpret the pattern in your life that has you stuck and to help ignite your purpose towards becoming who God created you to be! "Dare To Be You"!

F.L. Harrington Jr.

July 2015

Notes

Notes

www.ingramcontent.com/pod-product-compliance
Lightning Source LLC
LaVergne TN
LVHW011409080426
835511LV00005B/452